Adventure

Lake Powell-Glen Canyon Nat. Rec. Area • Navajo National Monument • Canyon de Chelly National Park • Monument Valley • Navajo Tribal Park • Goosenecks State Park • Natural Bridge National Monument • Mesa Verde National Park • Canyonlands National Park • Arches National Park • Goblin Valley State Park • Capitol Reef National Park • Grand Staircase-Escalante Nat. Monument • Dixie National Forest • Bryce Canyon • Cedar Breaks National Monument • Zion National Park • Pipe Springs National Monument • Grand Canyon Nat. Park-North Rim

This is a land of formations, be they a product of nature or humans building their way of life. Here we see the work of creation.

Throughout the Grand Circle rocks rise in a way of saying "we are here—come visit us". Follow your interests. Each family will find it's own adventure.

The Grand Cirle encompasses three states; Arizona, Colorado and Utah. And a nation—the Navajo Nation. Within this travel adventure lies the greatest concentration of federal and state parks, recreation areas and tribal lands in America. You could make this a week vacation (rushed!) or a month or more — your choice.

Front cover: A "circle" of areas seen within this book. Various photographers as credited throughout. Inside front cover: Monument Valley formations. Photo by David Muench. Page 1: Mesa Verde's Cliff Palace. Photo by Bruce Hucko. Pages 2/3: Sunset Arch at Grand Staircase-Escalante National Monument; Pages 4/5: Landscape Arch at Arches National Park. Photos by David Muench.

Edited by Mary L. Van Camp.
Book design by K. C. DenDooven.

Eighth Printing, 2008 • New Version

GRAND CIRCLE ADVENTURE: The Story Behind the Scenery
© 1994 KC PUBLICATIONS, INC.

*"in pictures... The Continuing Story" & Eagle Flag Icon
are registered in the U.S. Patent and Trademark Office.*

LC 94-075108. ISBN 0-88714-082-3.

GRAND CIRCLE ADVENTURE

THE STORY BEHIND THE SCENERY®

by Allen C. Reed

Allen Reed attended Colorado State College and the Los Angeles Art Center. He is a well-known freelance writer, photographer, and artist. This "hobby" has spanned a half century of servicing numerous publications with his considerable knowledge of and felling for America's great southwest.

No visit to the area is complete without a cruise uplake to the most sensational, naturally sculptured feature - Rainbow Bridge.

A Grand Circle Adventure—
For You to Enjoy

Gunsight Butte soars above Lake Powell in Padre Bay, halfway between Wahweap and Rainbow Bridge. In 1776, Spanish missionary-explorers Dominguez and Escalante and eight other expeditioners crossed the Colorado River just east of this towering rock monument.

ALLEN C. REED

This aerial view shows the immensity of the Glen Canyon Dam crossed by the seemingly slender Glen Canyon Bridge. The town of Page, Arizona, can be seen here in the background sitting high on a mesa overlooking the dam. Lake Powell, created when the dam became operational in 1963, was named in honor of Major John Wesley Powell, the first explorer through the treacherous Colorado River canyons. Nature decides the waterflow through the Colorado River system. During periods of "low water", a white line will show due to bleaching of the minerals from the canyon walls.

GARY LADD

From the *newest* (around 53 million years old) icing on the geological layer cake at Bryce Canyon and Cedar Breaks to the 2-billion-year-old exposed rock at the bottom of the Grand Canyon, our circle tour touches four different biogeographic zones. The span of these life zones reaches from the upper pine, spruce, and aspen forests of Bryce, Kaibab, Cedar Mountain, Boulder Mountain, and Mesa Verde down to the canyon-bottom Sonoran zone as found in southern Arizona and northwestern Mexico. With some overlapping, each zone supports its own variety of plant and animal life. Some of these higher zones, thrust up along the perimeter of the circuit, are always in sight, beckoning the traveler to enjoy an alpine side trip into a mountainous national forest.

The Grand Circle Adventure can start and end at any point of choice. The most practical approach is to start at the place most convenient for you, then set your own pace and enjoy.

STEVEN WARD

It's time for water fun at Lake Powell.
Everything that swims or floats seems to be present on the lake—from water skiiers pulled by powerboats to large cruisers and tour boats. A lot of watercraft can cruise a lake this size and not get in anyone's way.

Glen Canyon National Recreation Area

The modern, luxurious Lake Powell Resort and Marina near Glen Canyon Dam, the gateway to the water wonderland of Lake Powell, has become one of America's grandest lakeside resorts. Over 2 million visitors a year—from one or two vacationers up to full-fledged conventions—enjoy the many services it offers° in addition to the lodge itself such as the beach, campground, houseboat rentals and supplies, and daily tour boats to explore a variety of scenic adventures.

GARY LADD

At the center of our Grand Circle Adventure is the 1.25-million-acre Glen Canyon NRA with its center-piece—beautiful Lake Powell. This second-largest man-made lake in America is 186 miles long. Its meandering 1,960-mile canyon-serrated shoreline is longer than the combined shorelines of California, Oregon, and Washington.

The key commercial center of this remote recreation area is the town of Page, Arizona, on a mesa overlooking the dam. An hour or so spent at the Carl Hayden Visitor Center at the Glen Canyon Dam or at the John Wesley Powell Museum is an ideal way to start informing yourself about what this section of Grand Circle Adventure country is all about.

Page can be the gateway to still more delightful adventures in the area, such as a memorable one-day float trip on the Colorado River between towering 2,000-foot canyon walls. The starting point is beneath Glen Canyon Bridge, one of the world's highest steel arch bridges (700 feet overhead), located next to Glen Canyon Dam. The float ends 15 miles downriver at historic Lees Ferry.

The Glen Canyon Dam is an impressive sight. Both the exhibits at the Carl Hayden Visitor Center and a guided tour (offered May-October) or a year-round self-conducted tour through the immense power plant and inner workings of the dam are valuable experiences.

In 1963, Glen Canyon Dam was completed and became operational. The last generator was installed and dedicated in 1966, nearly ten years after the first construction began. The concrete arch rising 710 feet above bedrock holds back 27 million acre-feet of water at full-lake capacity. Inside, 600 feet down in an inner chamber, you will gaze upon a battery of eight immense whirring generating units spun by the escaping waters of Lake Powell. The maximum 1,124,000 kilowatts generated by this power plant, flowing to population centers like Las Vegas, Phoenix, Tucson, and smaller communities, is enough to supply continually a city of approximately 1 million residents.

One of man's mightiest engineering sculptures, Glen Canyon Dam was created to collect the waters from five rivers: the Colorado, San Juan, Dirty Devil, Escalante, and Green. The lake was named after the first of the pioneer Colorado River explorers, John Wesley Powell. Delightful glens, grand grottos, and majestic towering canyon walls inspired him to give Glen Canyon its name.

GARY LADD

On any summer day you can see recreationists taking full advantage of Lake Powell's offerings: sight-seeing, fishing, water skiing, or swimming.

On the lake every size of watercraft from inflatable neoprene vessels to 60-foot cruisers is represented; yet there is enough water space to offer a degree of privacy to almost everyone. A common sight arriving or leaving the Wahweap Marina are houseboats loaded with vacationers making their home on the water for a while.

In the midst of all this action, you can also just meditate. You can enjoy the drama of ever-changing moods of light and shadow on the vast backdrop of magnificently carved monuments and canyon walls that thrust hundreds of feet above the lake while they plunge brilliant color reflections equally as deep into the dark water below.

The multitude of bays on Lake Powell offer plenty of uncrowded play space. Close to a hundred winding isolated tributary canyons offer fascinating invitations to explore. Many narrow down until the walls brush both sides of even a small boat, leaving no choice but to back out in search of a wider place to turn around.

a **FEW** brown
(trout)
AT **MORE**
than 18 pounds

JOSEF MUENCH

JOSEF MUENCH

The crowning glory of a visit *to Lake Powell country is a trip to Rainbow Bridge, the largest known natural bridge in the world at 290 feet high. You can get there with your own boat, or on a regularly scheduled tour. To the Navajo, this "rainbow turned to stone" is most sacred. It may well impress you that way too, as its sheer elegance penetrates to the very depths of your soul. After its "discovery" by explorers in 1909, it was proclaimed a national monument by President Taft in 1910; however, due to its isolation was rarely visited until Lake Powell was established.*

For the rod-and-reel enthusiast there is year-round fishing for striped and largemouth bass, walleye, rainbow and brown trout, bluegill, sunfish, crappie, pike, and channel catfish. Stripers up to 31.5 pounds and crappie up to 3 pounds have been taken from Lake Powell. Below the dam, where the cold, deep lake water spills out through the penstocks and turbines into the Colorado River, it is not uncommon to pull in large trout. A few browns have been recorded at more than 18 pounds.

ALLEN C. REED

A *battery of 8 immense turbine-driven generators hum to the tune of several thousand cubic feet of water per second surging through 15-foor-diameter penstocks from Lake Powell. The maximum Glen Canyon Dam electrical production capacity is enough to supply a city of 1 million people. All this can be seen and is explained on tours that start and end at the dam's Carl Hayden Visitor Center.*

DAVID MUENCH

*E*ven without a boat, Lake Powell and the Glen Canyon NRA with its variety of things to do and its majestic scenic surroundings in all their dramatic moods can be the perfect vacation. Sometimes a simple hike along the shoreline can be the best way to relax.

Glen Canyon National Recreation Area cuts diagonally across the southeast corner of Utah. In just a few hours round trip, you can visit the Paria River canyon, vividly striped with as bright a spectrum of nature's geological coloring as can be found anywhere in the world.

In less than an hour by jeep from Page, you can walk in the quiet of the sandy floor of sculptured slot canyons. These wild exhibits of natural artistry, carved by centuries of periodic swirling flood waters, are a fantasy of sensational stone whirls and twists. These canyons are so narrow at the top that in some places you can step across.

No visit to the area is complete without a cruise uplake to the most sensational naturally sculptured feature of them all—the graceful 290-foot-high Rainbow Bridge.

Before Lake Powell backed up into Forbidding Canyon, Rainbow Bridge was inaccessible to all but a few hardy hikers. Today, the world's highest known stone bridge is just a few steps from a courtesy boat dock.

You can make the 48-mile trip from Wahweap Marina to Rainbow Bridge in your own boat, a rental boat, a chartered boat with guide, or on one of the many regular tour boats. However you go, Rainbow Bridge National Monument is an absolute must.

As sheep and wool are a main form of industry for the Navajo people, most Navajo children grow up around sheep. The girls are taught at an early age to help their mothers in cleaning, carding, dyeing, and spinning the wool into usable yarn for the weaving of the ever-popular Navajo rugs, prized for their quality and beauty. Often the preparation involved in getting the wool ready for weaving is longer than the actual weaving time. Most weavers execute a variety of patterns, at times depending on requests placed by traders. In summer the family lives and works in a covered shelter usually close to their hogan; however, if the best area for their sheep is farther away, they will move closer to the flocks. The Navajo way of life is a "family affair" with everyone working closely together. The Navajo is the largest Indian tribe in North America, with more than 180,000 living on their Reservation, "The Navajo Nation," in Arizona.

JERRY JACKA

Arches, monuments, and small ruins are isolated on the top or in the candy-striped canyons of White Mesa. Located just south of Arizona 98 between Page and U.S.160, it was named for its nearly white sandstone—a distinct contrast to the reds we are used to seeing in the Four Corners' area.

JERRY JACKA

In Navajo National Monument, three of Arizona's largest cliff dwellings—Inscription House, Betatakin, and Keet Seel—were once home for several hundred Anasazi (the "ancient ones"). Along with other prehistoric southwest dwellings, these were suddenly deserted around the close of the 13th century. A spectacular overlook of the 135-room Betatakin ruin 700 feet below is located near the Visitor Center and museum at Navajo National Monument. For enthusiasts of hiking, close-up photography, or Indian lore, regular ranger-guided descents offer access to the canyon floor.

DAVID MUENCH

Navajo National Monument

The next leg of your circuitous journey will be on Arizona 98, eastward across a section of the Navajo Reservation and past the tall stacks of the Navajo Power Generating Station. In the distance, that large blue-gray mound that seems to follow right along with you is 10,380-foot Navajo Mountain, a symbol sacred to the Navajo.

About 52 miles southeast of Page, a side road to the north is marked "Inscription House Ruin." This ancient Indian cliff dwelling of 74 units, part of the Navajo National Monument, was constructed sometime around A.D. 1274. After reaching U.S. 160, just 12 miles farther on, you travel another 13 miles north on 160 to intersecting Arizona 564. It is then just 9 miles on 564 to the Navajo National Monument Visitor Center.

Here a trail leads to an overlook above Betatakin (Beh-TAH-tah-kin), second of the three major ruins in the monument. The hike takes less than one hour round trip. This 135-room cliff dwelling is nestled in a 500-foot-high cave in the canyon wall opposite you.

If you want a more intimate look, scheduled ranger-conducted hikes will take you there. But be prepared for a three-hour round trip. Descending the 700 feet to the canyon floor is no problem—just so you remember that it will be uphill all the way back, at a breath-shortening altitude of over 7,000 feet.

The largest cliff dwelling in Arizona, Keet Seel, also is located in Navajo National Monument. Here there are 160 rooms and 6 *kivas* , (ceremonial cham-

ED COOPER

Canyon de Chelly's Spider Rock rises higher than an 80-story building, yet it could scarcely accommodate a one-room office on top. Traditional stories make this the home of Spider Woman who taught the Navajo women the art of weaving.

bers). It is a full day round trip to Keet Seel. To visit the cliff dwelling you must register at Park headquarters at least a day in advance, as visitation is limited. The primitive eight-mile trail to the ruin crosses the canyon stream numerous times. If all the arduous hiking with wet feet doesn't really appeal to you, horses and Navajo guides may be available.

Well-informed Navajo guides tell fascinating, and historical tales related to landmarks, and ancient ruins visited on four-wheel-drive inner-canyon tours. Canyon de Chelly's sheer and colorful sandstone walls soar a thousand feet to lock in a bountifully rich treasure chest of southwestern grandeur.

Canyon de Chelly

Returning to U.S. 160, turn northeast and proceed 19 miles to the Kayenta junction, then go 8 miles beyond it to Navajo Highway 59. Take Navajo 59 southeast 54 miles to U.S. 191 at Many Farms. From there it is 13 miles farther south to the Chinle turnoff and the mouth of Canyon de Chelly National Monument.

Here, evidence of the Great Pueblo period is profusely and dramatically represented. It is an awesome sensation to peer over a lofty canyon rim and gaze hundreds of feet down upon ancient multiroom dwellings or onto unique rock formations such as Spider Rock, ascending nearly 800 feet skyward from the placid canyon floor. "White House," "Antelope House," and "Mummy Cave" cliff dwellings are but a few exceptional examples of Canyon de Chelly's once-thriving early "residences" that were left behind by the end of the 13th century.

Near the Park headquarters, the highway splits, offering two splendid scenic rim drives. Navajo Highway 7, following the old Fort Defiance Trail on the south side of the canyon, leads to sensational overlooks from 500 to 1,000 feet above the floor of Canyon de Chelly, including the spectacular White House cliff dwelling and Spider Rock.

Navajo Highway 64 along the north rim leads to great views of Canyon del Muerto in the Canyon de Chelly monument and of ruins including a photographer's favorite Antelope House cliff dwelling.

The sandy canyon-bed prevents conventional car travel in the canyon. Heavy-duty four-wheel-drive commercial tour trucks with informative guides make travel into the canyon a delightful part of your visit.

JERRY JACKA

Mummy Cave
Ruin in Canyon del Muerto's principal tributary to Canyon de Chelly is one of the largest cliff dwelling in the area. Archaeological studies show this site to have been occupied over a thousand years—from the Basket Maker era to final desertion at the close of the Great Pueblo period.

The sandy streambed of Canyon de Chelly A is the roadless passageway for Navajo families
who live in and farm the canyon. These same elusive tracks are followed by four-wheel-drive tours that show visitors the canyon's innermost wonders. A border of venerable old cottonwoods adds a refreshing touch of summer green or shimmering gold in the fall.

To get to the next stop on the Grand Circle Adventure, you can backtrack to Kayenta junction, then travel 24 miles north on U.S. 163 to the Utah border and Monument Valley. If you wish to go to Mesa Verde National Park first, take U.S. 191 north then U.S. 160.

Monument Valley
Navajo Tribal Park

Drifting sand and towering stone spires like this Totem Pole and Yei-Bi-Chei Dancer formation make the setting that the Monument Valley Navajo call home. The proud and picturesque Navajo women in velveteen dresses with silver coin trim, and their famous turquoise jewelry add even more color to an already multihued land.

DAVID MUENCH

Travel into the Valley is confined to limited sections of dirt roads. To enjoy the innermost reaches, where you can experience the Valley at its best, to visit the Navajo at home (an octagonal dwelling called a *hogan*), and to learn what it is you are seeing and where you are at all times, your best bet is a four-wheel-drive tour. The licensed, well-informed guide is usually a Navajo who grew up in the area and who knows every arch, monument, and Navajo in the Valley. Tour information can be obtained at the tribal Visitor Center or at the Historic Goulding's Trading Post west of U.S. 163 on the Utah/Arizona border.

This mile-high monument-studded western scenic paradise is completely within the land of the Navajo. For the most part these gentle and hospitable people still lead a pastoral life as dry farmers and sheepmen. Their traditional cedar-log and mud-plastered hogans blend perfectly into the 1,500 square miles that make up Monument Valley.

Among Navajo women velveteen blouses in vivid blues, greens, yellows, purples, and reds and decorated with silver coins are still worn with equally colorful satiny ankle-length skirts. Treasures of

JOSEF MUENCH

The most famous early white settler in Monument Valley, Harry Goulding brought his young bride and dream to this then roadless, lonely land in 1923. He established the historic Goulding Trading Post, named many of the monuments, and befriended the Navajo. Later he introduced Monument Valley to the world by influencing Hollywood's John Ford to direct six major western epics there starting with Stagecoach in 1938.

DAVID MUENCH

An incongruous pair—windswept sand dunes and a trickle of water. Not a green leaf nor a blade of grass, but still a pleasant sight to thirsty Navajos and their sheep. Sand Springs, a rare phenomenon in semiarid Monument Valley, surfaces, flows a few paces, then returns to the sand.

handmade silver and turquoise jewelry adorn both Navajo men and women. The Navajo are well known as silversmiths and rug weavers.

In the inevitable, ever-changing pattern of progress, familiar old horse-drawn spring wagons, filled with picturesque Navajo families, and creeping along sandy ruts, have in many cases been replaced by pickup trucks, churning up cockscombs of dust on reservation roads or zipping along the hard-surfaced highways to Kayenta or Flagstaff.

Monument Valley is truly an artistic creation of nature, with its stately, photogenic carved red sandstone buttes and slender monoliths jutting into the sky and bearing names like "The Totem Pole," "The Three Sisters," "Rooster Rock," and the "Yei-B-ehei." Then there are the numerous wind- and weather-carved arches with descriptive names such as "The Sun's Eye," "Moccasin Arch," "Ear of the Wind," "The Great Hogan," and "Spider Web Arch."

The arches, monuments, and sand dunes of Monument Valley have made spectacular backdrops for scores of motion pictures beginning in 1938. In that year trading post operator Harry Goulding introduced John Ford to the Valley. Then John Wayne was brought in to star in *Stagecoach*. More major productions directed by Ford followed – *She Wore a Yellow Ribbon, Fort Apache, Cheyenne Autumn,* and *the Searchers.*

Hardly a season has gone by since 1938 without a movie or television commercial of some sort being filmed among the monuments.

Though the monuments we see have been slowly weathering away for millions of years since they were part of a vast upthrust ocean bed plateau, the change witnessed in a lifetime is so slight as to be imperceptible. However, there are occasions when in human presence the constant erosional process allows gravity to get the upper hand. This relentless force pulls down a great slab of stone, adding it to the talus slope and windblown sand while leaving on a canyon wall a fresh scar that was not there the day before.

But there is a Valley change readily visible, for it is almost sure to be a part of the daily routine. If the daytime scenario in Monument Valley is grand, the evening performance seldom fails to top it with an award-winning sunset sensation. Glowing monuments attempt to steal the scene while their shadows reach for miles across the sand, melting together at last to darken the entire valley floor.

Then comes the day's "grand finale." Night creeps up from the bases of the monuments to crowd the last orange rays of the sun off the tips of the already red sandstone buttes, firing them with an incandescence like molten copper that seems to radiate from within. Dusky monuments close the scene,

Moccasin Arch, one of many open formations in this valley full of arches, forms a sandstone halo above Monument Valley Navajos who enjoy being the colorful accents to their proud land. They willingly pose for visitors' cameras wearing their finest garments.

JOSEF MUENCH

Monument Valley: Spires, splinters, buttes, mesas, and arches. These eroded remnants from a distant past were given names of the living, spiritual, or material things of which they were reminiscent. To the Navajo, one line of stony figures depicts the sacred "Ye-Bi-Chei" ceremonial dancers. The "Big Hogan" arch is related to Navajo creation. To the white man the formations looked like: the North Window, the Rooster Rock, the Stagecoach, the Three Sisters, Half Moon Arch, Ford's Point, and even wearing apparel like these well-known Mittens.

JERRY JACKA

standing in silent silhouette against a varicolored violet, orange, and crimson sky. Night settling on the vast valley floor is disturbed only by a few visible, widely separated Navajo campfires. All is well for another day.

A masterpiece of nature and much more, Monument Valley is a pleasing blend of sight, sound, and tranquility, and of Navajo culture and legend. It is an experience not to be forgotten . . . ever!

ALLEN C. REED

Goosenecks State Park overlooks a series of tight switchbacks in the San Juan River. Deeply entrenched in its terraced depths 1,500 feet below, this canyon-locked river slowly and relentlessly carves its way to the upper end of Lake Powell.

Goosenecks State Park

From where the Goulding's-Monument Valley crossroad meets U.S. 163, it is 21 miles northeast on 163 to Mexican Hat, Utah, on the San Juan River, which in this area is the northern border of the Navajo Reservation. Just across the bridge over the San Juan, a traveler's oasis on the east side of the highway got its name, "Mexican Hat," from a strange stone formation resembling an inverted *sombrero*. A buckled anticline, or roof-shaped fold of stratified earth crust, in the background is called the *Raplee Anticline* or "Navajo Rug," after the weaving pattern it suggests.

About three miles farther north on U.S. 163, Utah 261 branches to the left, heading for Goosenecks State Park. A mile ahead on Utah 261 a marked turnoff (Utah 316) leads west three miles to a canyon rim overlooking the San Juan River, deeply entrenched in its erosion-terraced abyss 1,500 feet below. Here the river forms a series of tight "gooseneck" switchbacks as it meanders on its way to Lake Powell, transporting an estimated load of over 30 million tons of silt, sand, mud, and gravel each year. To complete this scene, a backdrop of Monument Valley monoliths serrates the distant skyline.

DICK DIETRICH

This inverted "Mexican Hat" on the San Juan River in southern Utah marks a resort area and starting place for scenic tours and float trips to Lake Powell.

JOSEF MUENCH

Monument Valley's Totem Pole and Yeibichai. These symbols of the Navajo Nation have great personal meaning to the Navajo people who live in the Valley.
Taken in 1937, this photo was the first color photo ever made by Josef Muench. Using Joe's photography, Harry Goulding, back in 1938, entied John Ford to shoot Stagecoach, the first western ever shot on location. It starred a young up-coming actor - John Wayne.
Be sure to visit the Goulding Museum at his Trading Post. Much of the human history of the Valley is shown, including film clips of movies and the early days. Even today Monument Valley serves as a continuing location for both movies and many automobile commercials.

Valley of the Gods *is an enchanting playground for both eye and camera. It takes little imagination to discover many sandstone-sculptured objects and animals. Near the entrance a huge organ grinder's monkey, complete with pillbox hat, welcomes you from a sleigh behind a Trojanlike horse. This 17-mile experience, just a little way off the beaten path, is a delightful adventure.*

ALLEN C. REED

Valley of the Gods

After you return to Utah 261, it is five and a half miles north to a right-hand turnoff marked "Valley of the Gods." This side road is a fair weather dirt loop 16 miles in length. The only sign of human habitation visible along this road is an old ranch house built by a grandson of Mormon pioneer and Colorado River ferryman John D. Lee (Lees Ferry).

The rest of the inhabitants of the valley are whatever your eyes make them out to be. For here is an enchanted playground for both the camera and your imagination. Sculptured stone columns and escarpments bring to mind objects from animals to stately "gods."

Where the Valley of the Gods loop road reaches U.S. 163, turn right, back toward Mexican Hat, four miles southwest. At the junction of U.S. 163 and 261, turn right on 261, this time bypassing both the Goosenecks and the Valley of the Gods turnoffs. You are on your way north to Natural Bridges National Monument. After Valley of the Gods, a left turn on U.S. 163 would take you to Bluff, Utah, and north.

You will not go far until you begin negotiating a series of hairpin switchbacks that elevate you several hundred feet to the crest of Cedar Mesa. If the switchbacks don't take your breath away, the view from an overlook near the top will. Below, the wide highway you have just traveled is but a thin thread

reaching for the horizon. Let your eyes follow it into the distance, and you will have a good idea of how well that often-used phrase "land of room enough and time enough" describes this part of the West.

Almost immediately after topping out on Cedar Mesa, you will encounter to the left a marked dirt road that leads five miles to Muley Point. Here is another spectacular lookout over a vast panorama of scoured-out San Juan canyon country, with the meandering river far below. As part of the Glen Canyon National Recreation Area, Muley Point provides an interpretive display on the geology of the area.

Natural Bridges
National Monument

Returning to Utah Highway 261 from Muley Point, you then drive north up the Moki Dugway and across the top of a grassy, juniper-covered plateau to Utah 95. The prominent twin buttes to the north are called the "Bears Ears." The Abajo Mountains to the northeast are in the Manti-La Sal National Forest. After going two miles west on Utah 95, you will then take Utah 275 for five miles to the Visitor Center and campground of Natural Bridges National Monument. This, the first National Park Service

Natural Bridges
National Monument protects three natural bridges carved out of sandstone, including the second and third largest in the world—Sipapu (220 feet high) and Kachina (210 feet high). Gold prospector, Cass Hite, came across these natural bridges in 1883 and, after his findings were reported and later publicized in "The National Geographic Magazine," the area was proclaimed a national monument by President Theodore Roosevelt in 1908. Here, the placid mirror reflection 167 feet below Sipapu Bridge offers no hint of this stream's alternate personality of raging storm-fed torrents that carved this massive formation.

DAVID MUENCH

area established in Utah, is open year-round.

A scenic nine-mile bridge-view drive from the Visitor Center takes in three massive natural bridges carved from Permian-age Cedar Mesa Sandstone. Viewing platforms overlooking each bridge are roughly 100 yards from designated parking areas. For hikers who feel the urge to explore further, miles of hiking trails connect all three of these natural wonders.

Two of the bridges, Sipapu and Kachina, exist in current streambeds—their abandoned stream meanders nearby. The third, Owachomo, on the side of the main streambed, is no longer scoured by streambed erosion but mostly by rain and frost action. Information on the bridges and the area is available at the Visitor Center. A campground is located nearby.

an **Enchanted** *playgound* for **BOTH** the *camera* **And Your** *imagination*

Overleaf: This stylized map drawn to approximate scale, sets forth the entire Grand Circle Adventure.

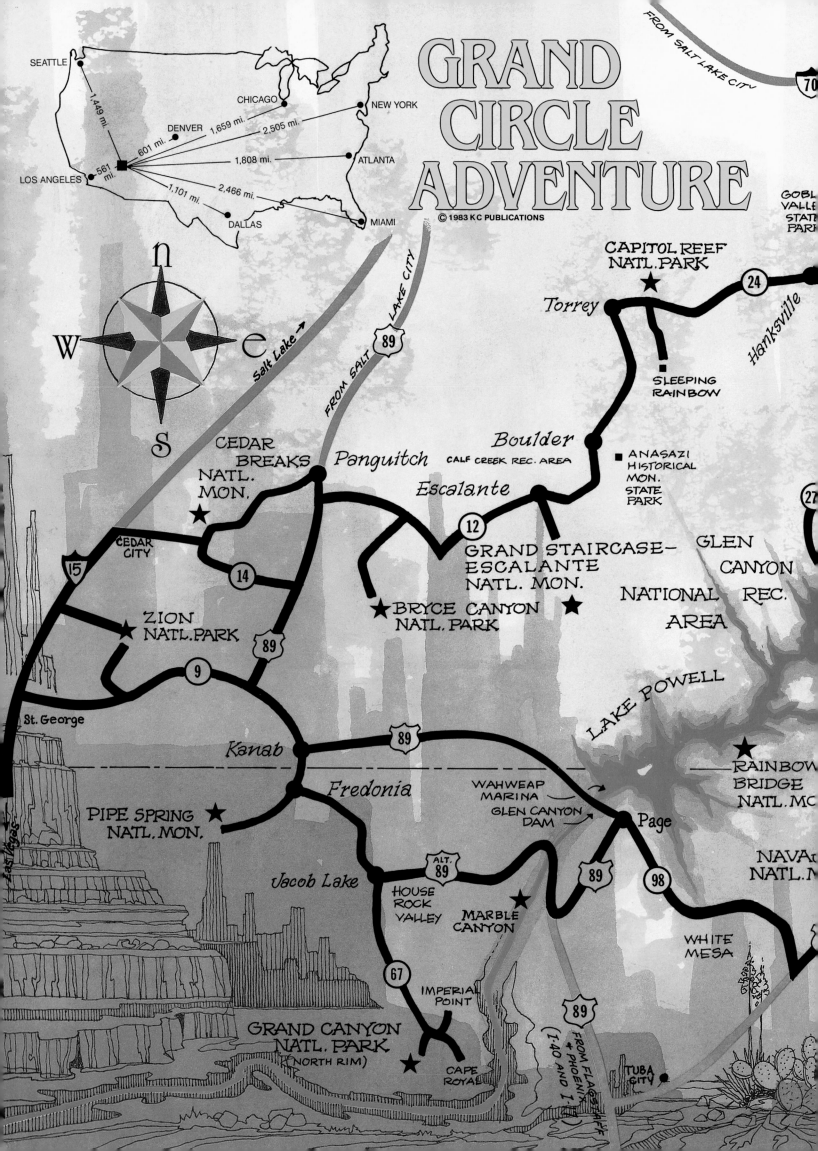

GRAND CIRCLE ADVENTURE

© 1983 KC PUBLICATIONS

SEATTLE

1,449 mi.

CHICAGO

NEW YORK

DENVER 1,659 mi.

2,505 mi.

601 mi.

1,808 mi.

ATLANTA

LOS ANGELES 561 mi.

1,101 mi. 2,466 mi.

MIAMI

DALLAS

FROM SALT LAKE CITY

70

GOBLIN VALLEY STATE PARK

n

W e

S

Salt Lake →

FROM SALT LAKE CITY

89

CAPITOL REEF NATL. PARK

Torrey

24

Hanksville

SLEEPING RAINBOW

CEDAR BREAKS NATL. MON.

Panguitch

Boulder

CALF CREEK REC. AREA

Escalante

ANASAZI HISTORICAL MON. STATE PARK

27

CEDAR CITY

14

12

GRAND STAIRCASE— ESCALANTE NATL. MON.

GLEN CANYON NATIONAL REC. AREA

15

ZION NATL. PARK

89

BRYCE CANYON NATL. PARK

9

LAKE POWELL

St. George

89

Kanab

RAINBOW BRIDGE NATL. MO.

Fredonia

WAHWEAP MARINA GLEN CANYON DAM

Page

PIPE SPRING NATL. MON.

East Vegas

Jacob Lake

ALT. 89

HOUSE ROCK VALLEY

MARBLE CANYON

89

98

NAVA NATL. M

WHITE MESA

67

IMPERIAL POINT

89

FROM FLAGSTAFF + PHOENIX (I-40 AND I

GRAND CANYON NATL. PARK (NORTH RIM)

CAPE ROYAL

TUBA CITY

Green River

70

FROM DENVER

70

Green River

★ ARCHES NATL. PARK

313

Moab

GRAND VIEW POINT →

DEADHORSE POINT STATE PARK

★ ISLAND IN THE SKY

191

CANYONLANDS NATL. PARK

NEEDLES DISTRICT ★

211

Colorado River

NEWSPAPER ROCK HISTORICAL MON.

■ HITE MARINA

Monticello

491

NATURAL BRIDGES NATL. MON. ★

Blanding

95

HALLS CROSSING MARINA

261

VALLEY OF THE GODS STATE PARK

262

★ HOVENWEEP NATL. MON.

Cortez

Durango

DENVER (I-25) →

160

MULEY POINT

GOOSENECK STATE PARK

Bluff

Mexican Hat

FOUR CORNERS

UTAH

COLORADO

★ MESA VERDE NATL. PARK

GOULDING LODGE TRADING POST ■

MONUMENT VALLEY

160

163

ARIZONA

NEW MEXICO

Kayenta

59

191

Many Farms

FROM FARMINGTON & ALBUQUERQUE · 25 + I-40

Chinle

CANYON DE CHELLY NATL. MON. ★

FROM FLAG.

LEGEND

GRAND CIRCLE ROUTE

PAVED ROADS

JOE WELLS

Of the scores of once-occupied mesa-top pueblos, most have crumbled under the relentless battering of the ages. Sun Temple, thought to be a carefully planned ceremonial structure, is one of the few surface ruins still partly standing. Built in the 1200s, it may never have been completed as there is no evidence that a roof covered the rooms.

JOSEF MUENCH

Mesa Verde National Park

Your trip through the Four Corners country cannot be considered complete without a visit to the majestic World Heritage Site, Mesa Verde National Park, and its matchless concentration of cliff dwellings. Mesa Verde is the classic example of prehistoric Anasazi Indian architecture, and it provides a most enlightening insight into how these people conducted their everyday life.

To reach Mesa Verde from Natural Bridges, you will return on Utah 275 to Utah 95, then proceed eastward on 95 for 31 miles. From here you will turn south on U.S. 191 for 22 miles to Bluff, then east and on to the town of Montezuma Creek and on to Aneth, Utah. At Aneth, a recently paved road takes you on a 40-mile drive towards Cortez, Colorado. Hovenweep National Monument is north of the highway—the Ancestral Puebloan sites are well worth taking the time to see. Approximately 8 miles east of Cortez on U.S. 160 is the entryway to Mesa Verde National Park. Road conditions are unpredictable due to rain or snow so it is wise to check with the state highway division or Mesa Verde National Park for current road information.

From the park entrance a 21-mile scenic mountainous roadway climbs over 1,600 feet while showing off distant desert topography and splendid vistas of six mountain ranges in four states. Lush farmland makes a crazy quilt of the Mancos River valley far below. From the 8,572-foot summit of Park Point, the road descends to the 6,900-foot level of the park headquarters area and leads to the Chapin Mesa Archeological Museum. At the museum you can obtain information about the prehistoric cliff dwellings and how best to see them.

At the park headquarters museum you can also marvel at the large collection of handsomely decorated pottery, baskets, tools, and other artifacts left behind when Mesa Verde's occupants moved away from the mesa around 700 years ago. A series of detailed dioramas depict the evolution of Ancestral Puebloan culture.

These dramatic displays, complete with inhabitants involved in their everyday way of life, can take the imagination back in time to when this civilization flourished. The time period illustrated by the dioramas ranges from the Basket Maker period of the 6th century through the Great Pueblo period from A.D. 1100 to 1300. The period during which the Ancestral Puebloan people built cliff dwellings lasted less than 100 years. It is thought that before the close of the 13th century severe drought and other causes drove these people from their homes forever, as it did the inhabitants at Hovenweep, the national monument you passed on the way here.

Fire !

Catastrophic wildland forest fires have been on the rise for the last ten years across the high-desert of the American Southwest. The lower canopy of a Pinyon-Juniper forest, typical in this part of the world, doesn't appear to the casual observer to have the same kind of potential to burn as its northern cousin; but looks can be deceiving. Several factors have to come together for a Pinyon-Juniper forest to ignite but once it does it is often a spectacular conflagration. Three factors determine how a fire will burn: the amount of fuel available, the topography of the land, and weather. Not only are fuel moistures lower in living trees and dead logs alike but drought stress causes trees to be more susceptible to a variety of infestations such as the Ips beetle. Dead and down trees increase the fuel load per acre and therefore the intensity of a fire. Hot, dry summers also increase the potential spread of fire. It's easy to be lulled into thinking that fire isn't a major threat in this part of the country but that just isn't the case.

NPS PHOTO BY JULIE A. BELL

Fire retardant or *Slurry, dyed red so pilots can follow their line on multiple drops, doesn't actually put fire out. It is used, often in conjunction with a fire break, to slow the spread of a fire and give firefighters a chance to combat a blaze.*

NPS PHOTO

Fortunately, *most alcove sites suffer relatively little damage from fire itself. Problems arise after the fact when the lack of vegetation above a site facilitates erosion. Mud and water often pour into alcove sites from above and damage fragile architecture.*

Circular subterranean "kivas"—a Hopi word for the rooms used as ceremonial structures—found in the ancient dwellings were entered by ladders through a roof hatchway like those in the stone-paved courtyard of Spruce Tree House, the third largest cliff dwelling Mesa Verde. A single dwelling may have several kivas—in this case 8—in order to accommodate its many residents. According to one belief, the various levels of the kiva represent stages in man's creation, with the roof and outdoors being the present world.

DAVID MUENCH

The largest and one of the best-preserved cliff dwellings in the Southwest is Mesa Verde's Cliff Palace. It is sheltered by an alcove 325 feet wide, 60 feet high, and 90 feet deep. Standing at the edge of a Mesa Verde cliff and looking down across a narrow canyon at Cliff Palace, you can imagine the thrill that cowboys Richard Wetherill and Charles Mason felt when they saw the cliff dwellings of Mesa Verde in 1888.

However, the height of fascination is likely to be the close-up experience of actually strolling through some of these well-preserved dwellings of the ancients with an informative Park Service ranger. There are scores of known sites in a variety of sizes and conditions preserved in the shielding cliff depressions of numerous mesa side canyons. Some of the better known and most often seen have descriptive names like "Square Tower House," "Spruce Tree House," "Long House," and "Balcony House." Ranger-guided ticketed tours will take you into a number of them. Along the roads of the mesa-top sites you can clearly see the sequence of prehistoric architectural development from pit houses to villages to cliff dwellings.

A visit to the museum, National Park Service information packets, foreign language guidebooks, road-side exhibits, guided and self-guided tours,

their GOLDEN AGE, only to be *Lost forever* at the CLOSE of the 13th century

and summer evening talks by rangers all contribute to the pleasure and understanding of the ancient inhabitants of this 52,000-acre park area. Food, lodging, camping, and bus tours are available in the park from early May to late October. The park headquarters and museum are open every day of the year, even throughout the winter months.

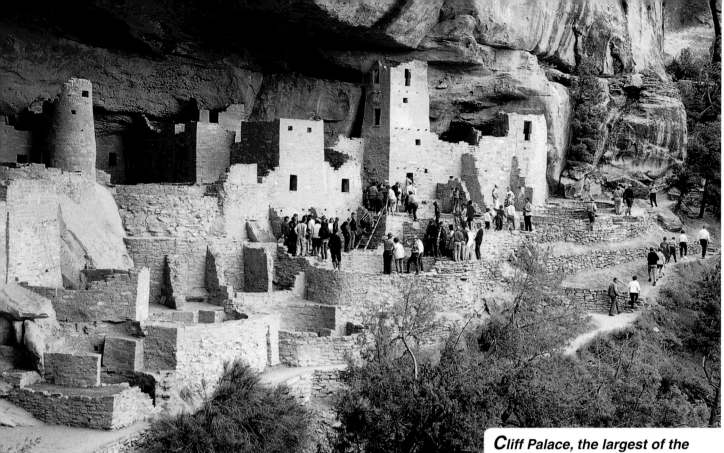

Cliff Palace, the largest of the preserved Mesa Verde cliff dwellings, is a classic example of Great Pueblo culture. Its 200 rooms and 23 clan kivas were once a part of the life style of over 200 people. Here in the cliff dwellings and mesa-top pueblos, refinements in architecture, farming, pottery, and textile weaving reached their "Golden Age," only to be lost forever when the mesa was completely and inexplicably deserted at the close of the 13th century.

Storage rooms were built at the back of the caves, and the family rooms toward the front, with the kivas the farthest forward. Not all parts of the dwelling had ceilings, as where the top of the cave was high enough it served as the roof of the highest story. The Prominent four-story structure that dominates Square Tower House was not originally a tower. Second- and third-story walls of adjoining dwellings have fallen away, leaving this tallest Mesa Verde ruin to stand alone.

Angel Arch in Canyonlands

TOM TILL

National Park's Needles District, has been a focal point of the Park since its establishment in 1964. Named by visitors to the area in 1953, it was no doubt viewed long before that by cowboys who herded their cattle through the rugged country seeking the hard-to-find grass and water needed for subsistence.

Canyonlands National Park—Needles District

To reach the Needles District of Canyonlands National Park from Mesa Verde, return to Cortez, Colorado, then take U.S. 491 north. For these next 60 miles the highway passes through rolling farmland on the way to Monticello, Utah, which is 22 miles north of Blanding. Nearly 15 miles north of Monticello on U.S, 191, a lone light-colored Entrada Sandstone butte with a red sandstone base juts up on the east side of the road. This is "Church Rock," sometimes referred to as the "Wine Jug" because of its juglike shape, with an imaginary little bit of red wine left at the bottom.

On the opposite side of the highway from this lone landmark, Utah 211 leads west through 38 miles of scenic canyon country to the "Needles District" in the southern section of Canyonlands National Park.

About 12 miles in, the roadway passes one of the best-preserved and most intriguing collections of petroglyphs in the Southwest. This flat Wingate Sandstone formation known as "Newspaper Rock" is a State Historical Monument. Aged with a blackened coat of natural mineral stain (manganese oxide) called "desert varnish," it is covered with hundreds of impressions pecked into its surface. It is estimated that the numerous inscriptions and figures cut into the sandstone cliff probably span a thousand years. They include figures made by prehistoric Indians and those made more recently by Utes and a few early white settlers.

As you head west through a variety of colorful canyon formations, along the last 19 miles into the Needles area two historical landmarks, North and

Known as the "North and South Windows," this formation in Arches National Park is also called "The Spectacles." Let your imagination roam wild and see whatever you will here in nature's spectacular gallery of monuments.

South Sixshooter peaks, are plainly visible on the skyline. Another unusual sandstone formation against the skyline farther on is a fairly good replica of a giant wooden shoe. Approximately 32 miles from U.S. 191 you reach the park boundary.

The drama of Canyonlands National Park, with its surrealistic 525-square-mile maze of meandering canyons, swirls of candy-striped sandstone fins, bristling forests of towering monoliths, gravity-defying balanced rocks, and graceful arches could be billed as "300 million years in the making." It is an explorer's utopia by foot, river, air, or four-wheel-drive vehicle.

A short distance into the park is the Visitor Center, which provides information about the area, trails, campground, and other facilities. It is not far from here to the highway's end amid a cluster of colorful spires and pinnacles—outposts of the vast, mysterious badlands beyond.

If standing on the outside looking in is not enough, and you are physically up to it, you can load your backpack with necessary supplies—maps, water, camera and film—and hike in.

The best bet is a four-wheel-drive vehicle, but the going can be rough with some 40 percent grades and switchbacks. Elephant Hill is still one of the great challenges to four-wheel drivers. However, your rewards will be many, for hidden throughout

these canyons are scores of fantastic natural formations. Names of some of the better known, like "Angel Arch, "Devil's Lane," and "Paul Bunyan's Potty," may offer some descriptive clues to their bizarre appearance.

The easiest way to obtain an overall view, is to arrange for a scenic flight. Local inquiries at the Needles Outpost and at Moab and Monticello should lead to some interesting adventures in this treasure trove of wild and wonderful banded sandstone formations.

Arches National Park

When you return from the Needles District of Canyonlands National Park to U.S. 191, you will drive 39 miles north to Moab, Utah. Located on the Colorado River, this community is a next door neighbor to Arches National Park. Moab is one of the largest business-supply centers on this Grand Circle Adventure. At an elevation of 4,000 feet, Moab Valley is rich in scenery, minerals, and signs of the prehistoric past—from dinosaur tracks embedded in sandstone to Ancestral Puebloan sites. From here you can arrange for a float trip down the Colorado River—another way to come to know this powerful country.

The gateway to Arches National Park is approximately six miles north of Moab on U.S. 191.

Turret Arch is another example of the major formations of salmon-colored Entrada Sandstone visible in Arches National Park. On sparkling-clear summer days it is hard to imagine the violent forces of water and ice erosion that combined to create this magical land. Spires, pinnacles, and balanced rocks perches atop seemingly inadequate bases join with the arches as scenic wonders for the enjoyment of visitors to this rugged red rock country.

JOSEF MUENCH

Arches National Park contains one of the greatest density of arches in the world. These formations were created by water, extreme temperatures, and underground salt movement. There are more than 2,500 catalogued arches ranging in size from a 3-foot opening (which is the minimum considered an arch), to the majestic proportions of Landscape Arch, which measures 306 feet from base to base. Delicate Arch, shown here, stands on the brink of a canyon with the dramatic La Sal Mountains in the background.

JEFF GNASS

What is the magic that holds Balanced Rock in place? While geologists would tell us that it is calcium carbonate that cements the sand grains together, others prefer to think in terms of a moment in time when gravity hasn't quite won—yet!

DAVID MUENCH

A paved highway takes you to viewpoints and trail heads from which hikers can reach the most spectacular of the over 2,500 arches in this 119-square-mile gallery of nature's magnificent masterpieces. Again the elements have run rampant—sculpturing, balancing, and painting majestic murals.

Visualize a slim, graceful horizontal stone span, chiseled from an enormous sandstone "fin" over 300 feet long, weighing thousands of tons, and tapering down to a thickness of a mere 12 feet in the middle. This is Landscape Arch, one of the longest known natural arches in the world. To stand in its presence—but not *under* it, as rocks have fallen in recent history—requires an easy mile hike from a parking area. But take along a wide-angle lens if you want to get both ends in your picture. The well-constructed trail to Landscape Arch, and one more mile beyond, rewards the hiker with views of six natural arches.

Another fascinating arch, just steps away from a parking area, is Double Arch. The larger of the two openings could accommodate a 15-story building with room to spare.

Perhaps the best known and most photographed formation in Arches National Park is Delicate Arch. This majestic natural wonder can be observed in the distance from a viewpoint on the east side of the park. However, the most spectacular view of it requires a somewhat demanding mile-and-a-half hike that climbs 500 feet from the historic Wolfe Ranch area of the park. John Wesley Wolfe, a Civil War veteran, homesteaded this ranch in 1898. Today, a time-worn log cabin, a corral, and the remains of a wagon are all that is left by the side of the trail to Delicate Arch.

It would be difficult to surpass the stately splendor of Delicate Arch as it stands alone, both feet planted firmly on the crest of its own private sandstone amphitheater. But when the nearby La Sal Mountain range is snowcapped behind this majestic red sandstone frame, and when sun and sky and clouds act out their roles, the ultimate in nature's dramatic artistry is unveiled.

Arches National Park is open to visitors year-round as are lodging and supply centers in Moab. On your trip to Arches don't miss the Visitor Center, which offers a wealth of interesting geological, historical, and general information about the area.

Dead Horse Point State Park

After returning from Arches to U.S. 191, you will travel only 6 miles north before you encounter Utah 313 to your left. Approximately 14 miles west of this turnoff, the marked, paved highway continues southeast 22 miles to Utah's Dead Horse Point State Park.

Dead Horse Point overlooks a magnificent sweep of spectacular canyon lands including a loop in the Colorado River nearly 2,000 feet down. The erosion-terraced canyon walls expose layer upon layer of sandstone, mudstone, conglomerate, and limestone formations laid down between 200 and 300 million years of intermittent overflow and departure of shallow inland seas. Relentless natural forces of erosion took their time in carving the terrain below as the river washed thousands of cubic miles of rock, silt, and sand sediments into an ancient sea.

Just before arriving at the tip of Dead Horse Point, the highway passes through a narrowed neck that almost isolates the point from the rest of the plateau. In the early days of western settlement, bands of wild horses that roamed the plateau were driven toward the point by local cowboys. A short fence across the narrow strip was all that was needed to trap the horses in a natural corral between the sheer cliffs until the better ones could be sorted out and sold. As the story goes, one band of horses corralled too long died for lack of water, thus creating the name that this promontory still carries.

Where the highway enters the park you will find a Visitor Center, a museum and a developed campground. On the horizon the distant La Sal Mountains provide a splendid background.

Canyonlands National Park— Island in the Sky District

On your way back from Dead Horse Point, take the road to your left. It leads to the "Island in the Sky District" of Canyonlands National Park. You can view the north section of this park from a 6,000-foot-high bench plateau separating the Green River and the Colorado River canyons.

Over millions of years relentless natural forces of erosion carved the terracelike canyon scene spread out beneath Dead Horse Point. A gooseneck loop in the Colorado River is nearly 2,000 feet straight down. A thread of the four-wheel-drive Shafer Trail, constructed during the uranium boom of the 1950s, meanders below.

The Visitor Center at the park entrance will provide maps and information on trails, campground, and points of scenic interest. (Come prepared, as there is no water available in the Island in the Sky District.)

Some of the more prominent features are "Green River Overlook" and "Upheaval Dome." "Grand View Point" at the far southern tip of the plateau overlooks a vast gouged-out basin of red organlike rock spires and cliffs capped with White Rim Sandstone reminiscent of sugar icing on a chocolate cake. In the distance the Needles District of Canyonlands lies almost due south of Grand View Point. After having absorbed the wild beauty of this remote area, return along Utah 313, then proceed north to U.S. 191 and drive 21 miles north to where U.S. 191 meets Interstate 70.

Goblin Valley State Park

West on 1-70, 35 miles, Utah 24 heads south to the Goblin Valley area on its way to Hanksville. About 25 miles south on Utah 24, a paved road marked "Goblin Valley State Park" intersects from the west. Five miles in on this road a signed, paved road heading southwest takes you to the last seven miles to a wide secluded valley. Its hard-packed, sunbaked floor is populated with thousands of standing rocks of Entrada Sandstone, sculptured by nature and resembling almost every type of goblinlike creature your wildest imagination will allow.

The Island in the Sky District of Canyonlands National Park is a broad, level mesa sandwiched between the Green and Colorado rivers. About 1,200 feet below the Island is the White Rim, a nearly continuous sandstone bench, and another 1,000 feet down are the rivers. Washer Woman Arch is a spectacular formation found in the Island District, and may be viewed by hikers from the Mesa Arch Trail.

TOM TILL

JOSEF MUENCH

*E*rosion plays many whimsical tricks. Here in the Fisher Towers area, not far from Arches National Park, an imaginary dinosaur rears its fierce stony head.

ALLEN C. REED

*H*undreds of "little people" and their strange pets keep watch on your every move in Goblin Valley.

Strolling amidst the goblins' grotesque forms, you can easily lose hours discovering and photographing. There are giants over 50 feet tall down through man-size to stony little trolls. There are those with long noses and those with short noses— some stand alone, while some are apparently seriously engrossed in conference. And there is no shortage of their stony pets—animals from caterpillars to Donald Duck. Goblin Valley is a name well chosen for this fascinating fantasyland where you and your camera will have a field day.

Although there are a few four-wheel-drive roads in the area, there is not much choice for a conventional car but to backtrack to Utah 24, then turn south for 20 miles and cross the Dirty Devil River to Hanksville en route to Capitol Reef.

From Hanksville you can take an interesting side trip southeast on Utah 95 to Hite Marina at the upper end of Lake Powell. Beyond Hite would take you back to Natural Bridges and Monument Valley.

Capitol Reef National Park

West from Hanksville, Utah 24 follows the scenic Fremont River canyon past several marked points of historical interest 30 miles to the colorful towering cliffs and deep canyons of Capitol Reef National Park. In 1937, 3,700 acres were set aside as Capitol Reef National Monument. It was not until 1971 that an act of the U.S. Congress enlarged the boundaries and changed its status to that of a National Park.

Capitol Reef is a sensation in geological formation, color, history, and wildlife. Some people have called this canyon country "Land of the Sleeping Rainbow", because the variegated outcrops of geologic formations that stretch like a sprawling rainbow along the base of the cliffs. The name of this 241,271-acre park was inspired by massive grayish-white domes eroded from a layer of Navajo Sandstone 1,000 feet thick. These forms were thought to be reminiscent of the dome of the nation's Capitol.

The 726-foot steel arch on Utah 95 at Hite crosses the Colorado River arm of Lake Powell 141 miles uplake from Glen Canyon Dam. Gold prospector, Cass Hite, originally named this "Dandy Crossing" as it was the best place to ford the Colorado above Lees Ferry. The region around Hite is perhaps the most scenic in Glen Canyon NRA. On the way to Hite from Hanksville is the turnoff, Utah 276, to Bullfrog Marina.

JEFF GNASS

The "Reef" part of the park's name was applied to the massive barrierlike "S"-shaped upthrusted fold in the earth's crust called the "Waterpocket Fold." This description term comes from numerous natural tanks and potholes that hold huge quantities or rainwater in the spring. The extreme subterranean pressures that wrinkled the earth's crust into the fold exposed the edges of at least fourteen different layers of geological formations, laid one on top of another, over a period of 275 million years. This gigantic upheaval of majestic domes, sheer multicolored escarpments, and deeply eroded canyons extends nearly 100 miles from the north end of the park south beyond the Bullfrog Basin section of Lake Powell.

Visitors can spend days hiking the local trails or making side trips into a variety of nearby scenic and historic locations. Places with highly appropriate or historic names include "Cathedral Valley," "Capitol Gorge," "Cohab Canyon," "Cassidy Arch," and "Golden Throne."

Zane Grey's novel *Robber's Roost* was inspired by the maze of blind canyons and hidden trails in this remote area, once a favorite haunt of Butch Cassidy, "The Sundance Kid," "Big Nose" George Curry,

and the rest of the "Wild Bunch." These notorious Old-West outlaws used this rugged canyon country as an escape route or as a hideout after relieving a bank, train, or mine paymaster of cash on hand. Knowing intimately every trail and water hole in these badlands made eluding even a knowledgeable posse a simple matter. A number of books and movies have been produced to immortalize this setting. Some of the better-known novels, in addition to *Robber's Roost*, are Pearl Baker's *The Wild Bunch*, and Charles Kelly's *The Outlaw Trail*. Paul Newman and Robert Redford helped keep the legends alive in the movie *Butch Cassidy and the Sundance Kid*. The old homestead cabin in which Butch Cassidy grew up still stands about 60 air miles west of the Visitor Center near Circleville, Utah, on U.S. 89.

JEFF GNASS

A magnificent extravaganza of wild geological display and vivid color—that is Capitol Reef National Park. From the regal splendor of Cathedral Valley, majestic domes, towering cliffs, mysterious canyons, and hidden pools stretch 70 miles south to Lake Powell's Bullfrog Basin.

The golden rewards of fall colors are evident throughout the "Land of the Sleeping Rainbow" that is Capitol Reef National Park. Proclaimed a national monument in 1937, Capitol Reef protects remote and rugged landscapes. Its status was changed to that of a national park in 1971.

DAVID MUENCH

The Capitol Reef Visitor Center on Sulphur Creek is a lush oasis in this rather barren canyon country. The center is located in a verdant valley of pastureland and fruit orchards walled in by towering cliffs. This site was farmed by early Mormon pioneer families.

Dixie National Forest

Ten miles west of Capitol Reef on Utah 24, there is a turnoff just before you come to the town of Torrey. From here Utah 12 (Boulder Mountain Road)—paved and open year-round—offers a scenic drive into the north side of the Grand Staircase-Escalante on the way to Bryce Canyon.

The first 38 miles, to the quiet farming community of Boulder, pass through part of the Dixie National Forest and across scenic, forested Boulder Mountain—9,200 feet high at its summit. In spring and summer the grassy meadows are a sea of wildflowers. Golden aspen shimmer among dark stately pines in fall.

JOSEF MUENCH

The Capitol Reef area is loaded with historical remnants of a pioneer past, like this weathered old mill near Teasdale, Utah.

- 38 -

Boulder, with a population of less than 100, is a delight to see. At the north edge of Boulder are the Anasazi Indian Village State Historical Monument and a museum. A collection of artifacts and information makes a visit here well worthwhile in helping round out your knowledge and understanding of the prehistoric Indian culture that occupied the Colorado Plateau country so many centuries ago.

A Visitor Center at Escalante will introduce you to this new Bureau of Land Management and Escalante area.

Grand Staircase-Escalante National Monument

The Grand Staircase-Escalante National Monument under the jurisdiction of the Bureau of Land Management was established in 1996. It is one of the largest designated public lands in America.

Here for you is two million acres (7,540 square kilometers) of canyons, sheer rock walls, forests, and about 1,000 miles of open roads. This place represents both nature's fantacies and the pioneer spirit of humans for thousands of years.

You will find evidence of early man preceeding any known tribe - early mormon settlers and today's rugged individuals, who live and enjoy their unique way of life. To see the inner parts ot the Escalante you need a good four-wheel drive vehicle and a survivors attitude. For the more casual visitor there are still many locations to see.

There's the drive along Highway 12, north of the Monument, towards Bryce Canyon. The southern west to east route, Highway 89, goes from Kanab, Utah to Page, Arizona. Both will give you a good feel for this remarkable country.

At Escalante, Cannonville, Kanab and Big Water (on U.S. 89), the BLM has visitor centers. They can tell you current road conditions which can change daily! This is a vast country (about the size of Delaware and Rhode Island combined!)

From Boulder, Utah, before you come to Escalante, a well graded, but un-paved road leads to the Hole-In-The-Rock overlook. Mormon pioneers in 1879 did the impossible by moving wagons, livestock, entire families down an almost verticle 2,000 foot drop off.

Out of Escalante a connecting north-south route (Road 300), the Smoky Mountain Road, takes you across a narrow ridge with spectacular views. Four-wheel drive suggested.

From Henrieville, just before Cannonville, the Cottonwood Road (#400) is a reasonably well maintained graded route. Along the way are two remark-

BLM PHOTO BY P. ANDERSON

Cottonwood Canyon Road snakes through the upper end of the Cockscomb south of Grosvenor Arch. This dirt road was constructed in the 1960's in conjunction with the power line that brought electricity north to the small communities of Bryce Valley. Now, it allows vehicle access through the interior of the Monument to northern gateway towns of Cannonville, Tropic, Henrieville, Escalante, and Boulder

K.C. DENDOOVEN

Sandstone into dramatic freeform goblins, monoliths, and gravity-defyingspans such as Metate Arch. Behind the arch—midway down the ivory-colored layer—a second, smaller, arch is beginning. The Monument's landscape is a work in progress, an unceasing process of tearing down and building up.

able stopping spots. Grosvenor Arch and Kodachrome, a Utah State Park.

What you will see in the Grand Staircase-Escalante depends on how much time you allow. Want to see it all? Plan on at least two weeks minimum just to cover the basic roads and trails.

Indian pictographs and rock writing are seen in many locations. Unique shapes, arches and natural bridges are in many locations. Petrified wood is found. One specimen is six feet in diameter and 90 feet long. Along the way you will pass working cattle ranches—this is a land of many uses.

Remarkable as this place is, we have to move on. So, from along Highway 12, after you visit the pioneer museum in Cannonville, Route 12 will take you through Tropic, up to the turn off into Bryce Canyon National Park.

DAVID MUENCH

Bryce is really two different worlds—a heavily *forested 8,000-foot plateau and, below the rim, a wonderworld of hundreds of formations such as this Queen Victoria sculpture.*

ED COOPER

A 19th-century government surveyor called Bryce *Canyon "the wildest, most wonderful scene the eye of man ever beheld." To a geologist the Pink Cliffs of Bryce were "a brilliant jewel in a land of superb texture and workmanship." Paiute Indians saw the stony sentinels as "red rocks standing like men in a bowl-shaped canyon."*

Bryce Canyon National Park

Bryce Canyon received its name from an early Mormon pioneer, Ebenezer Bryce, who settled in the area, built a cabin, and claimed grazing rights. According to folklore, his best-remembered description of Bryce Canyon was: "A hell of a place to lose a cow!" Because he ran cattle in the area, his statement probably carried a note of authentic, firsthand experience.

Until you park your car at the visitor center and walk to the rim of the canyon, you are in a ponderosa, spruce, fir, and aspen forest typical of this 8,000-foot altitude. Then, when you emerge from the forest at the edge of the Pink Cliffs, you face a vast expanse of delicate, intricately eroded, multicolored minarets, spires, and pinnacles that, by the thousands, make up the lacy fretwork of the striking badland topography below.

Most of the geological formations you have seen so far on this adventure were carved from solidified sands and sediments laid down 250 to 125 million years ago. Comparatively, Bryce Canyon

National Park is a rank newcomer, dating back a mere 60 million years.

To set the first stage, powerful subterranean forces thrust the surrounding land up causing watercourses to drain inland, dumping a wide variety and vast volume of silt and mud sediments into huge inland lakes. The buoyancy of the water provided a natural sorting process. Larger, coarse materials dropped out first where the rivers entered the lakes. In the deepest water a limy ooze of finer silts and clays settled to the bottom. Centuries of deposition compressed these sediments into limestone.

Later, with more intermittent regional shifting, a final uplift of the present Bryce area drained the lakes for the last time and exposed the solidified sediments. More shifts of the earth's crust followed, along with ever-present erosion from rain, snow and ice. This relatively soft, less stable material was broken and sculptured into the delicate, colorful columns that make Bryce Canyon the exotic expression of nature's art that it is today.

Regularly scheduled horseback trips with qualified wranglers may be arranged at Bryce Canyon. The ride winds deep into an enchanted stone forest of ethereal brilliance—an exciting, never-to-be forgotten adventure.

There are a number of rim-drive viewpoints of these pastel-tinted monuments. In addition, a series of trails invites you to wander down among the delicately carved corridors and palisades of the inner canyons. But if the altitude of Bryce seems a little high for extended hikes, you can take one of the horseback trips conducted during the summer season.

Cedar Breaks National Monument

The next trail on your adventure leads 21 miles northwest, via Utah 12 and U.S. 89, down 1,000 feet through the pines, silver-green sage, and bluffs of Red Canyon to Panguitch, Utah. From Panguitch, Utah 143 climbs 3,000 feet to an altitude of 10,000 feet in the Dixie National Forest. The highway skirts Panguitch Lake and winds 32 miles through majestic forests of pine, spruce, and quaking aspen and through rolling green mountain meadows—all of which are garnished with wildflowers during spring and summer.

You have slipped into Cedar Breaks National Monument by the "back door" on the north end. When you arrive at the canyon rim, you will find a gigantic multihued amphitheater spread out at your feet. Although the origin, composition, and coloring of Cedar Breaks are much the same as those of the Pink Cliffs of Bryce Canyon, you will find that this entire ten-square-mile monument has a physical character, a personality, and a beauty all its own.

Here, as in many other areas of the West, the juniper trees were erroneously referred to as "cedars" by the early settlers. This misnomer, combined with their common use of the word "breaks" in referring to badlands, resulted in the "Cedar Breaks" name.

Standing north of Highway 14, is the fantastic cluster of limestone forms known as "Cedar Breaks," a name given to the area by early settlers who mistook the juniper trees for cedars and referred to the steep badlands as the "breaks." This richly colored amphitheater lies along the western face of the Markagunt Plateau. Less well known than Bryce Canyon, its counterpart to the east, Cedar Breaks exhibits much the same geologic story, although its scenic vistas are uniquely its own.

At the east side of Zion, Checkerboard Mesa is a dramatic of nature at work. It's all from the effects of the scouring wind; from ice freezing and thawing; and from the release of pressures from within.

Leaving Cedar Breaks by the southern route (Utah 148) you can turn east on Utah 14, 23 miles back to U.S. 89, or west on Utah 14 to Cedar City, Utah, and 1-15. South on 1-15 takes you to Zion National Park. Your first encounter will be the Kolob unit of Zion, then south on 1-15 to Utah 17 and 9 takes you into the heart of Zion. If you went east on Utah 14, at Long Valley Junction you would meet U.S. 89. It is then 22 miles south to Mount Carmel Junction. From here Utah 9 travels west 23 miles to Zion National Park, This approach to Zion meanders through immense sandstone formations that originated millions of years ago as gigantic wind-deposited sand dunes that were later covered and compressed into stone. They will give you a modest clue as to what is to be seen in the park.

Zion National Park

En route to Zion Canyon, the road goes through two tunnels, one more than a mile long. Just before the second and longer tunnel, on the right (or north) side the Canyon Overlook Trail leads up a half mile to a magnificent view of the west side of Zion and the looping ribbon of the Zion-Mount Carmel highway far below. It is an interesting, easy walk to this point and well worth the hour round trip.

After passing through the long tunnel and driving down the winding loops that you saw from the overlook, you will encounter to the right the Zion Canyon turnoff that follows along the North Fork of the Virgin River for six miles. This road will take you to the Zion Lodge. Beyond the lodge a few miles the road terminates in a parking area deep in the bottom of the canyon. However, if you continue on a short distance past this turnoff straight ahead on the main park road, you will come to Zion's Visitor Center. All travelers should plan to stop here as the center offers area maps, information, and exhibits on geology, natural history, and other topics related to the park. During much of the year, illustrated interpretive talks on the Park are presented each evening at the lodge and campgrounds.

Unlike the more fragile, ornamental spires of Bryce, Zion is overwhelmingly massive and seems to engulf the valley below. When you tour this Park you can see a great deal right from the highway. Tree-framed impressions of immense erosion-carved

- 43 -

Heavy stands of evergreen and quaking aspen rise past expansive flower-decked meadows all the way across the Kaibab Plateau right to the edge of the Grand Canyon's North Rim. Here they frame the colorful array of buttes, temples, and mesas thrusting up from the gorge far below.

JOSEF MUENCH

sandstone formations thrusting hundreds of feet upward are viewed from different perspectives at every turn. Nature's colorful megaliths, with names like "Great White Throne," "Court of the Patriarchs," "Mountain of the Sun," "The Sentinel," and "Angels Landing" tower over the highway on the canyon floor.

As you stand deeply immersed in admiration of the Zion scene, the relentless drama of erosion goes on imperceptibly right before your eyes. It is estimated that at present the Virgin River removes more than a million tons of rock and sand from the canyon each year. The major portion is transported during extensive snowmelt or massive thunderstorm-caused flooding.

Complementing the Park's striking views and points of interest are many hiking trails. There are nearly a dozen maintained trails, rated from easy to strenuous, which lead to East Rim, West Rim, Emerald Pools, Weeping Rock, Hidden Canyon, Angels Landing, Watchman Viewpoint, and Sand Bench.

Pipe Spring National Monument

Leaving Zion, you drive east on Utah 9 to Mount Carmel Junction and U.S. 89, then continue south on U.S. 89, 17 miles to Kanab, Utah.

Kanab is an early Mormon settlement. It is well worth spending a little time driving along a few back streets and looking at some of the picturesque architecture of fine old southern Utah homes.

Just seven miles south of Kanab on U.S. Alternate 89 (89A), which crosses the border into Arizona, is the town of Fredonia. Here Arizona 389 cuts off to the west 14 miles to Pipe Spring National Monument on the Kaibab-Paiute Indian Reservation.

In 1870, Mormon leader Brigham Young established a ranch at Pipe Spring for raising cattle and production of dairy products. A stone-block fort was built at Pipe Spring to protect the ranch workers and their families. This picturesque, well-preserved historic Mormon fort served as a ranch house until 1923, when it was made a national monument in recognition of the early Mormon settlers.

Grand Canyon National Park—North Rim

Returning to Fredonia, you head south on U.S. 89A toward the world-renowned Grand Canyon of Arizona, 73 miles away. The highway soon starts its climb of nearly 3,000 feet to Jacob Lake, a popular wayside stop for tourists who are hungry or needing a tank of gas.

From the Jacob Lake highway junction, Arizona State Highway 67 heads south through 44 miles of evergreen and aspen forests and wide mountain meadows to the North Rim of the Grand Canyon. You will not know that the canyon is there until you get out of your car and take a few steps through the trees. Suddenly you are standing on the rim of an immense, deep, plunging chasm with towering sun-tinted rock forms-one of nature's greatest wonders.

This incredible canyon, 10-16 miles in width, was scoured out of a mile-thick series of sedimentary rock layers by all the forces of nature's elements— heat, cold, ice, sand, roots, earth tremors, and gravity. For millions of years they have worked in close harmony with the abrasive, silt-laden Colorado River. Tributaries bring debris eroded from a 150,000-square-mile area. It is estimated that before construction of Glen Canyon Dam, in one day at high flood stage the Colorado carried over 235,000 tons of the rasping rock, sand, and silt that gouge the canyon walls along the way.

More than a dozen geologic layers are visible at the Grand Canyon. To the casual observer these colorful stratified formations are a work of art. But to the geologist they are much more. In biting deeply into the earth's crust, *time* and the *river* have exposed the orderly pages of an illustrated text. Each layer, with its telltale fossils and composition, illustrates the geologic stairway that life on earth climbed through the ages.

The Kaibab Plateau slopes southward; thus water from rain and snow deposited on the northern rim drains *into* the canyon. On the South Rim much of the water flow is also southward, *away* from the canyon. Therefore, the north wall recedes more sharply, leaving the river channel closer to the South Rim. An additional contribution to variation in canyonside erosion is the 25-inch average annual rainfall on the north side versus 16 inches for the south. If there are eight or ten feet of snow on the North Rim, it is likely that snowfall measures four or five feet on the South Rim and that there is little or none at the bottom of the canyon.

The lone buttes and mesas in the sea of space

DICK DIETRICH

The brilliant, lush greenery of summer enhances this view of Cape Royal and Angel's Window at the North Rim of the Grand Canyon. In all parts of the canyon the ever-changing weather moods and seasonal changes offer a never-the-same variety of scenery for visitors.

between canyon walls have been gnawed free from ancient rim areas by eroding side canyons that eventually joined, isolating former portions of the Kaibab Plateau.

As you look across the canyon you will see on the far side the forested South Rim, approximately 1,000 feet below you. By trail it is 14 miles from the North Rim to the Colorado River and 7.8 miles more to South Rim Village. It is less than 22 miles on foot or by mule, 9 miles by air, but more than 200 miles by car. Two additional North Rim viewpoints reached by park roads are Cape Royal and Point Imperial.

Six North Rim trails, ranging from a third of a mile to 12 miles in length, and the 14-mile Bright Angel Trail down to the Colorado offer hikers a variety of workouts. If you have time, the best way to round out your Grand Canyon experience is to see it from the inside out by taking a one-day muleback ride down the trail to Roaring Springs.

Here is our recreation area, for millions to enjoy each year. On a map this lake becomes the diagonal through the center of this Grand Circle Adventure. As you travel these routes keep in mind—it's all about water—the force that created monuments, canyons, bridges, arches, rivers and the magnificent Lake Powell. Enjoy!

MARC MUENCH

Return to Our Starting Point

After you have left the grandeur of the North Rim, you will drive back via Arizona 67 to the Jacob Lake junction. From there U.S. 89A winds down from the forested Kaibab Plateau eastward onto the wide sweep of House Rock Valley. Seventeen miles east of Jacob Lake a dirt side road leads about 22 miles to a buffalo range where a protected herd wanders with the freedom they enjoyed a hundred years ago.

Back on U.S. 89A, as you skirt the base of the lofty Vermilion Cliffs on your way northeast, you will spot a tiny oasis hugging the base of the cliffs, called Cliff Dwellers Lodge. This little haven was developed by northern Arizona pioneer Art Greene and his family. The Greenes later established the first marina on Lake Powell, just across the Glen Canyon Dam from Page, Arizona.

A few miles farther east at Marble Canyon, steel-girdered New Navajo Bridge crosses the walled-in Colorado River, 467 feet below. The bridge is just four miles downriver from historic Lees Ferry.

On the east side of the bridge the highway reenters the Navajo Reservation. Fourteen miles beyond the bridge, 89A joints U.S. 89, which, turning northward, ascends the Echo Cliffs. From their crest you can see the vast panorama of the valley you have just crossed. The Kaibab National Forest looms dark on the distant skyline. Below, the Colorado River cuts a ragged gash through Grand Canyon National Park. As U.S. 89 slices through a deep notch at the crest of this red escarpment, you are now on the home stretch. From here it is only 20 miles back to our starting point at Lake Powell.

There are scores of additional things to see and do throughout this entire "linger-a-while" land—far too many to do justice to in the space allotted here. Each Park, each monument, each place has its own personality . . . its own character . . . its own individual charm. In seeking out the many historic and scenic landmarks, you will have the added enjoyment and pleasure of personal discovery when you take the *Grand Circle Adventure*.

Grand Circle Adventure

Contact Us

Page-Lake Powell
Chamber of Commerce
608 Elm Street, Suite C
P O Box 727
Page, AZ 86040
(928) 645-2741
(928) 645-3181 fax

Kayenta Chamber of Commerce
P.O. Box 187
Kayenta, AZ 86033
(520) 697-3463

Cortez Chamber of Commerce
928 East Main
PO Box 968
Cortez, CO 81321
970-565-3414

Moab Area Chamber of Commerce
217 East Center Street, Suite 250
Moab, UT 84532
(435) 259-7814
(435) 259-8519
info@moabchamber.com

Escalante Chamber of Commerce
P.O. Box 175
Escalante, UT 84726
escalante@escalante-cc.com

Kanab Chamber of Commerce
78 South 100 East
Kanab, UT 84741
(800) 733-5263

SUGGESTED READING

The following books are published by KC Publications, with selected titles available in translation packages (see our web site).

ALLEN, DIANE AND FREDERICK, LARRY. *in pictures Arches & Canyonlands: The Continuing Story*. Las Vegas, Nevada: KC Publications, 1993.

BEZY, JOHN. *Bryce Canyon: The Story Behind the Scenery*. Las Vegas, Nevada: KC Publications, 1980.

COLCLAZER, SUSAN. *in pictures Bryce Canyon: The Continuing Story*. Las Vegas, Nevada: KC Publications, 1989.

DAVIES, DENNY. *in pictures Glen Canyon—Lake Powell: The Continuing Story*. Las Vegas, Nevada: KC Publications, 1992.

DENDOOVEN, K.C. *Monument Valley: The Story Behind the Scenery*. Las Vegas, Nevada: KC Publications, 1992.

EARDLEY, A. J. AND SCHAACK, JAMES W. *Zion: The Story Behind the Scenery*. Las Vegas, Nevada: KC Publications, 1991 (rev. ed.).

EVERHART, RONALD E. *Glen Canyon-Lake Powell: The Story Behind the Scenery*. Las Vegas, Nevada: KC Publications, 1983.

HUNSAKER, JOYCE B. *Grand Staircase Escalante: The Story Behind the Scenery*. Las Vegas, Nevada: KC Publications, 2005.

JACKSON, VICTOR L. *in pictures Zion: The Continuing Story*. Las Vegas, Nevada: KC Publications, 1989.

JOHNSON, DAVID W. *Arches: The Story Behind the Scenery*. Las Vegas, Nevada: KC Publications, 1985.

JOHNSON, DAVID W. *Canyonlands: The Story Behind the Scenery*. Las Vegas, Nevada: KC Publications, 1989.

LADD, GARY. *Landforms—Heart of the Colorado Plateau: The Story Behind the Scenery*. Las Vegas, Nevada: KC Publications, 1995.

LADD, GARY. *Rainbow Bridge: The Story Behind the Scenery*. Las Vegas, Nevada: KC Publications, 1998.

MARTIN, LINDA. *Mesa Verde: The Story Behind the Scenery*. Las Vegas, Nevada: KC Publications, 1993.

MURPHY, DAN. *John Wesley Powell, Voyage of Discovery: The Story Behind the Scenery*. Las Vegas, Nevada: KC Publications, 1991.

OLSON, VIRGIL J. & HELEN. *Capitol Reef: The Story Behind the Scenery*. Las Vegas, Nevada: KC Publications, 1990 (rev. ed.).

RUDD, CONNIE. *Grand Canyon-North Rim: The Story Behind the Scenery*. Las Vegas, Nevada: KC Publications, 1989.

SUPPLEE, CHARLES AND ANDERSON, DOUGLAS & BARBARA. *Canyon de Chelly: The Story Behind the Scenery*. Las Vegas, Nevada: KC Publications, 1990 (rev. ed.).

www.kcspeaks.com

The Grand Circle; an Adventure
300 million years in the making

JOHN P. GEORGE

Delicate Arch, in Arches National Park, and the snow capped La Sal mountains sum up this entire adventure. Scenic beauty, the forces of Nature, crisp clean air—this land awaits you.

KC Publications has been the leading publisher of colorful, interpretive books about National Park areas, public lands, Indian lands, and related subjects for over 45 years. We have 6 active series—over 125 titles—with Translation Packages in up to 8 languages for over half the areas we cover. Write, call, or visit our web site for our full-color catalog.

Our series are:

The Story Behind the Scenery® – Compelling stories of over 65 National Park areas and similar Public Land areas. Some with Translation Packages.

in pictures... Nature's Continuing Story™– A companion, pictorially oriented, series on America's National Parks. All titles have Translation Packages.

For Young Adventurers® – Dedicated to young seekers and keepers of all things wild and sacred. Explore America's Heritage from A to Z.

Voyage of Discovery® – Exploration of the expansion of the western United States.

Indian Culture and the Southwest – All about Native Americans, past and present.

Calendars – For National Parks in dramatic full color, and a companion Color Your Own series.

To receive our full-color catalog featuring over 125 titles—Books, Calendars, and other related specialty products:
Call (800-626-9673), fax (702-433-3420), write to the address below, or visit our web sites at www.kcpub.com and www.kcspeaks.com

Published by KC Publications, P.O. Box 3615, Wickenburg, AZ 85358

Inside Back Cover: Sunrise over Lake Powell, the day awakes Photo by David Muench

Back Cover: Monumen Valley's Totem Pole and Yei-bi-cha As timeless as the Navajo people Photo by John P. George

Created, Designed, and Published in the U.S..
Printed by Tien Wah Press (Pte.) Ltd, Singapo
Pre-Press by United Graphic Pte. L